DOE-HDBK-1131-98
December 1998

Change Notice No. 1
November 2003

**Reaffirmation with
Errata
April 2004**

DOE HANDBOOK

GENERAL EMPLOYEE RADIOLOGICAL TRAINING

U.S. Department of Energy
Washington, D.C. 20585

AREA TRNG

April 2004 Reaffirmation Changes to DOE-HDBK-1131-98, General Employee Radiological Safety

Section/page/para	Change
Part 1, page 8	Revised "Training Records" to read: Training records and course documentation shall meet the requirements of 10 CFR 835.704 "Administrative Records" and be in accordance with local DOE Records Disposition Schedules.
Part 1, A-9	Under In-Field Observation, at end, add: Awareness drills, such as placing mock radioactive material in an unauthorized location to assess responses are also effective.
Part 2, page 6 and part 3 page 8	Under "Man made sources…" deleted domestic water supply and revised 1st sentence to read: Man-made sources of radiation, where the radiation is either produced or enhanced by human activities, contribute to the remainder of the annual average radiation dose (approximately 60 millirem).

Foreword

This Handbook describes an implementation process for core training as recommended in Implementation Guide G441.12A, *Radiation Safety Training,* and as outlined in the *DOE Radiological Control Standard* [RCS – DOE-STD-1098-99]. The Handbook is meant to assist those individuals within the Department of Energy, Managing and Operating contractors, and Managing and Integrating contractors identified as having responsibility for implementing core training recommended by the RCS. This training is intended for general employees to assist in meeting their job-specific training requirements of 10 CFR 835. While this Handbook addresses many requirements of 10 CFR 835 Subpart J, it must be supplemented with facility-specific information to achieve full compliance.

This Handbook contains recommended training materials consistent with other DOE core radiological training materials. The training material consists of the following documents:

Program Management Guide - This document contains detailed information on how to use the Handbook material.

Instructor's Guide - This document contains a lesson plan for instructor use, including notation of key points for inclusion of facility-specific information.

Student's Guide - This document contains student handout material and also should be augmented by facility-specific information.

This Handbook was produced in WordPerfect 9.0 and has been formatted for printing on an HP 4M (or higher) LaserJet printer. Copies of this Handbook may be obtained from either the DOE Radiation Safety Training Home Page Internet site (http://tis.eh.doe.gov/whs/rhmwp/rst/rst.htm) or the DOE Technical Standards Program Internet site (http://tis.eh.doe.gov/techstds/). Documents downloaded from the DOE Radiation Safety Training Home Page Internet site may be manipulated using the software noted above.

This page intentionally left blank.

General Employee Radiological Training

Program Management Guide

Coordinated and Conducted
for
Office of Environment, Safety & Health
U.S. Department of Energy

This page intentionally left blank.

Course Developers

Christine Liner	Savannah River Site (Development Chairperson)
Al Reeder	Lockheed Martin Energy Systems
Carolyn Owen	Lawrence Livermore National Laboratory
Dean Atchinson	Brookhaven National Laboratory
Brent Pearson	Coleman Industries
Roland Jean	Sandia National Laboratory
Karin Jessen	Lockheed Martin Energy Systems

Course Reviewers

Technical Standards Managers	U.S. Department of Energy
Peter O'Connell	U.S. Department of Energy
William Ulicny	ATL International, Inc.

This page intentionally left blank.

Table of Contents

This page intentionally left blank.

Introduction

Purpose and Scope

This handbook describes the DOE General Employee Radiological Training program. It includes standards and policies as well as recommendations for material development and program administration. It is intended for use by DOE contractors for the development of facility-specific general employee radiological training.

Compliance with 10 CFR 835-Subpart J

The DOE core training materials for General Employee Radiological Training (GERT) reflect the requirements identified in 10 CFR 835-Subpart J, "Radiation Safety Training" and recommendations identified in the DOE Implementation Guide G441.12A, *Radiation Safety Training,* and in the *DOE Radiological Control Standard* [DOE-STD-1098-99]. When implemented in its entirety and supplemented as noted with appropriate facility-specific information, this handbook is an acceptable method to meet the requirements of 10 CFR 835-Subpart J for general employee radiological training. However, it is incumbent on management of each facility to review the content of this handbook against the radiological hazards present to ensure that the training content is appropriate to each individual's prior training, work assignments, and degree of exposure to potential radiological hazards.

Training described in this handbook does not eliminate the need for additional training for facility-specific hazards. Notations throughout the program documents indicate the need for facility-specific information. If the noted section is not applicable to the facility, no information is required to be presented. The site Radiological Control Manager or designee should concur in facility-generated radiological training material.

Goal of Training Program

The goal of the core training program is to provide a sufficient level of knowledge and skills in radiological fundamentals commensurate with the assigned duties and potential radiological hazards encountered as a general employee at DOE facilities using or possessing radioactive materials and/or radiation-producing devices.

Organizational Relationships and Reporting Structure

1. DOE Office of Worker Protection Policy and Programs (DOE EH-52) is responsible for approving and maintaining the core training materials associated with the GERT program.

2. The establishment of a comprehensive and effective contractor site radiological control training program is the responsibility of line management and their subordinates. The training function may be performed by a separate training organization, but the responsibility for quality and effectiveness rests with line management.

Training Program Description

Overview of Training Program

General Employee Radiological Training (GERT) is provided to all site employees who receive occupational exposure during access to controlled areas (as defined in 10 CFR 835.2(a)) at a DOE site or facility or who are permitted unescorted access to controlled areas. These individuals may routinely enter the controlled areas and encounter radiological barriers, postings, radiation producing devices or radioactive materials. Employee responsibilities for observing and obeying radiological postings and procedures are emphasized throughout this training.

- Additional training beyond GERT is required for employees who are identified as radiological workers. Every employee, both radiological worker and non-radiological worker, must play an active part in maintaining exposures to radiation and radioactive materials within DOE limits and As Low As Is Reasonably Achievable (ALARA).

- GERT qualified individuals should be able to place the risks associated with working at a nuclear facility in perspective with other risks that we take in our everyday life.

Description of Programs

GERT Core Academic Material is approximately 1 hour in length, but will vary dependent upon the amount of facility-specific material.

GERT Core Academic Training includes the following:

Sources of Radiation, Non-ionizing and Ionizing Radiation, Risks in Perspective, Radiological Controls, Monitoring (Dosimetry), Emergency Procedures, ALARA Program, Employee Responsibilities for the ALARA Program, and Exposure Reports.

Proficiency Requirements

In accordance with 10 CFR 835-Subpart J, each individual shall complete training on the topics established in 10 CFR 835-Subpart J, commensurate with the hazards in the area and required controls, prior to being permitted unescorted access to controlled areas and prior to receiving occupational exposure during access to controlled areas at a DOE site or facility. An examination or performance demonstration is not required.

Retraining

In accordance with 10 CFR 835-Subpart J, training shall be provided to individuals when there is a significant change to radiation protection policies and procedures that may affect the individual and at intervals not to exceed 24 months.

Training should include selected fundamentals of the initial training with emphasis on seldom-used knowledge and skills. Training should be tailored to subjects for which trainee evaluations and experience indicate that special emphasis and depth of coverage is needed.

A self-study method may be used, when possible, for retraining. A suggestion for a self-study method is to allow the workers to self-study the training material followed by a presentation of any updates or changes, lessons learned, etc.

DOE recommends that, in the alternate year when training is not required, the GERT handbook be provided to general employees.

Materials developed in support of training should be document-ed in accordance with 10 CFR 835.704 "Administrative Records."

Instructor Training and Qualifications

All classroom instruction should be provided by instructors qualified in accordance with the contractor's site instructor qualification program. Training staff (contractor and subcontractor, if used) should possess both technical knowledge and experience, and the developmental and instructional skills required to fulfill their assigned duties.

1. Training staff responsible for program management, supervision, and development should have and maintain the education, experience, and technical qualifications required for their jobs.

2. Instructors should have the technical qualifications, including adequate theory, practical knowledge, and experience, for the subject matter that they are assigned to teach.

3. Methods should be in place at each contractor site to ensure that individual instructors meet and maintain position qualification requirements.

4. Subject matter experts without instructor qualification may provide training in their area of expertise. However, if these subject matter experts are to be permanent instructors, they should be trained as instructors in the next practical training cycle.

DOE Order 5480.20A, "Personnel Selection, Qualification, and Training Requirements for DOE Nuclear Facilities," discusses qualification requirements for instructors.

Training Program Material Development

Training Material Presentation

Training materials for the core programs consist of lesson plans and study guides. To ensure compliance with 10 CFR 835-Subpart J, facility-specific materials must be added to the core materials when necessary to adequately train individuals for facility-specific radiological hazards.

Training Certificates

A training certificate that identifies the individual's current training status may be provided to qualified personnel. Each facility is responsible for administering and tracking the certificates. Facilities have the option of utilizing the certificates as proof of training.

However, it should be noted that 10 CFR 835-Subpart J requires each facility to ensure general employees have adequate training for the hazards present. The training certificate from another DOE site does not, in itself, relieve the facility from ensuring the worker has had adequate training. It is appropriate for facilities to supplement a visiting employee's training with facility-specific training sufficient to ensure an adequate level of training for the hazards present.

Training Aids, References

Facility-specific training aids may be developed at the facility to suit individual training styles. Each facility may add information, activities, and/or view graphs to enhance the program.

Training Program Standards and Policies

Lectures, Seminars, Training Exercises, etc.

> GERT core training programs are designed to be delivered in a classroom setting. An alternate delivery method may be implemented with computer-based training (CBT) equipment or web-based training (WBT) equipment. The presentation of GERT should include core materials and facility-specific information.

Delinquent Training/Failure Procedures and Policies

> General employees who are delinquent on retraining shall lose their status of having unescorted access to controlled areas until successful completion of the delinquent training requirement.

Exceptions and Waivers

> Successful completion of the core course for GERT training at one DOE site may be recognized by other DOE sites. However, the determination as to the adequacy of training as required by 10 CFR 835-Subpart J is the responsibility of the facility in which the general employee will have access to, or receive occupational exposure in, controlled areas.

Administration

Training Records

> Training records and course documentation shall meet the requirements of 10 CFR 835.704 "Administrative Records" and be in accordance with local DOE Records Disposition Schedules.

Training Program Development/Change Requests

> All requests for program changes and revisions should be submitted to EH-52 using the DOE Technical Standard Program form "Document Improvement Proposal" F 1300.3. This form is available from the DOE Technical Standards Home Page - Maintenance of DOE Technical Standards TSPP-09). See the Foreword of this document for website address.

Audits (internal and external)

> Internal verification of training effectiveness may be accomplished through senior instructor or supervisor observation of practical applications and discussions of course material. Results should be documented and maintained by the organization responsible for Radiological Control Training. The GERT core training program materials and processes will be evaluated on a periodic basis by DOE-HQ. The evaluation should include a comparison of program elements with applicable industry standards and requirements.

Evaluating Training Program Effectiveness

> Verification of the effectiveness of Radiological Control training should be accomplished by surveying a limited subset of former students in the workplace. This evaluation should include observation of practical applications and discussion of the course material, and may include an associated written examination. DOE/EH has issued guidelines for evaluating the effectiveness of radiological training through the DOE Operations Offices and DOE Field Offices. These guidelines are included as an attachment to this Program Management Guide.

> For additional guidance, refer to DOE STD 1070-94, "Guide for Evaluation of Nuclear Facility Training Programs." The guidelines contained in these documents are relevant for the establishment and implementation of post-training evaluation and retention testing programs.

In response to Defense Nuclear Facilities Safety Board (DNFSB) Recommendation 91-6, DOE committed to develop an implementation plan to upgrade radiation protection programs at DOE defense nuclear facilities.

The implementation plan detailed DOE's plans to develop and implement radiation protection post-training evaluation and retention testing programs. Post-training evaluations will be used to identify opportunities for improving course materials and instruction methods and techniques and the need for additional training. Retention testing will indicate when individual performance or testing fails to meet expectations. Corrective actions for deficiencies identified in retention testing will be incorporated in the individual's development plan and the site's training program on an appropriate schedule.

In addition, Article 613.7 of the DOE Radiological Control Standard states that sites should implement a training effectiveness verification program. This program, which is in addition to performance evaluations routinely performed by the site's training department, is to verify the effectiveness of radiological control training by surveying a limited subset of former students in the workplace. This recommendation applies to both DOE defense nuclear facilities and DOE facilities not classified as defense nuclear facilities.
Per DOE's commitment to DNFSB, it is expected that all defense nuclear facilities will implement these or equivalent programs. DOE facilities not classified as defense nuclear facilities should also strive to implement such programs. Line management should monitor progress of program implementation.

The guidance provided in DOE STD-1070-94 is not meant to be prescriptive. Training organizations should review this guidance and determine its applicability, taking into consideration the existence of similar programs already in place at their facilities.

Forward evaluation results indicating a possible need to revise core training programs to EH-52 using the "Request for Change to DOE Core Training Materials" form.

References and Supporting Documents

Cohen, Bernard L., "Catalog of Risks Extended and Updated," Health Physics, the Radiation Protection Journal, Vol. 61, 1991.

NCRP, "Ionizing Radiation Exposure of the Population of the United States," Report No. 93.

ORAU 88/H-99, "Guide to Good Practice in Radiation Protection Training."

Scinta Inc., Radiological Health Handbook, 3rd Edition 1998

Travis, E. L., "Primer of Medical Radiobiology," 1989.

U.S. Department of Energy, Implementation Guidance for Use with 10 CFR 835, "Occupational Radiation Protection." DOE G 441.12A, "Radiation Safety Training."

U.S. Department of Energy, DOE Order 5480.20A, Ch. 1, "Personnel Selection, Qualification, and Training Requirements for DOE Nuclear Facilities," July ,2001.

U.S. Department of Energy, DOE STD 1070-94, "Guide for Evaluation of Nuclear Facility Training Programs", Reaffirmed 1999.

U.S. Department of Energy, DOE-STD 1098-99, "DOE Radiological Control Standard", 1999.

U.S. Department of Energy, "Occupational Radiation Protection," 10 CFR 835, November 1988.

U.S. Department of Energy, "Reproductive Health: Effects of Chemical and Radiation on Fertility and the Unborn Child," Lawrence Livermore National Laboratory, February 1, 1984.

U.S. Nuclear Regulatory Commission, "Instruction Concerning Prenatal Radiation Exposure," U.S. NRC Regulatory Guide 8.13, December 1987.

U.S. Nuclear Regulatory Commission, "Instruction Concerning Risks From Occupational Radiation Exposure," U.S. NRC Regulatory Guide 8.29, Version 1, February 1997.

ATTACHMENT

EVALUATING THE EFFECTIVENESS OF RADIOLOGICAL TRAINING

REV 1, 1998

Guidelines to Establish and Conduct a Program and a Retention Testing
Program Post-Training Evaluation

This page intentionally left blank.

TABLE OF CONTENTS

This page intentionally left blank.

I. INTRODUCTION

In response to Defense Nuclear Facilities Safety Board (DNFSB) Recommendation 91-6, DOE developed the following guidelines to support efforts to upgrade the Department's radiation protection programs. These guidelines support implementation of the U.S. Department of Energy "Radiological Control Standard," Article 613.7 (1999).

A. Purpose

The purpose of a training program and its associated evaluation phase is to assure that workers are qualified to perform their jobs competently and safely. This purpose should be kept foremost while establishing the procedural controls of the post-training evaluation process at each site.

The purpose of this document is to aid DOE sites in developing procedures and practices for conducting post-training evaluation and retention testing of the following core radiological control training courses: GERT, RW, and RCT training. Similar procedures and practices should be applied to post-training evaluation and retention testing of the supplemental radiological control training courses.

A retention testing program differs from a post-training evaluation program in the usage of its results. The results of a retention testing program are used to assist in: (1) identifying when individual performance fails to meet expectations; (2) identifying adverse trends in radiological performance; and (3) correcting individual performance deficiencies. The results of a post-training evaluation program are directed towards improving the training program rather than correcting individual performance deficiencies.

This document provides guidance on the issues and practices that should be considered in setting up such programs. It is not intended to prescribe specific practices that must be followed by all sites.

The diversity of conditions among the various DOE sites will require that the application of good practices recommended in this guideline may differ from site to site. That diversity includes the nature of the training organization, the nature of the trainees, the number of trainees, and the frequency in which the trainees will apply the training.

The conduct of evaluations will require that evaluators be trained at each site. In particular, the consistency with which any set of evaluators will rate the skill and knowledge levels of the former trainees will need to be emphasized. It is essential that the judgement of skill levels not vary appreciably from one evaluator to the next. The expertise needed to conduct such training may be available at the site or may be acquired from offsite sources. Several written references are provided.

The results of post-training evaluations may be used to upgrade core course materials as described in the Program Management Guides.

B. <u>Purpose of Post-Training Evaluation and Retention Testing</u>

Post-training evaluation has four primary purposes:

1. To measure the retention of skills and knowledge provided during training for extended periods following the training;
2. To measure the degree to which the training is used on the job;
3. To provide feedback to improve the training; and
4. To measure the cost effectiveness of the training.

A primary purpose of retention testing is to incorporate corrective actions into individual development plans based on deficiencies observed during the retention testing process.

C. <u>Assumptions</u>

1. These guidelines will be specific to evaluation of the radiological control training contained in the core training materials.
2. The applications of these guidelines will be unique for each DOE site.
3. Each DOE site will formalize its Radiological Safety Training Post-Training Evaluation Program and Retention Testing Program in site procedures.
4. These guidelines summarize the requirements of other documents, which explain more fully the process of training evaluation.
5. These guidelines are sufficient for knowledgeable individuals to use to create site controlling procedures.
6. Personnel engaged in post-training evaluation or retention testing will require some training or previous evaluation experience.
7. Individual sites may choose to include this evaluation program as part of site-wide evaluation of training.
8. Other radiological control training may be considered for evaluation along with core training.
9. The phrase "in the workplace" in the RCS cited below is taken figuratively to mean at the work location. While observation of skills would be preferable while engaged in real work at the actual workplace, the discussion of content may or may not be best done at that location. Written testing would be best done in a classroom setting where quiet and privacy may be maintained.

D. <u>Guidance From DOE-STD-1070-94</u>

DOE-STD-1070-94, "Guidelines For Evaluation of Nuclear Facility Training Programs," appendix A, objective 8.0, "Training Program Evaluation," contains seven criteria. Three of these criteria are applicable to the purpose of these guidelines:

Criteria 8.1: A comprehensive evaluation of individual training programs is conducted by qualified individuals on a periodic basis to identify program strengths and weaknesses.

Criteria 8.3:   Feedback from trainee performance during training is used to evaluate and refine the training program. Feedback from former trainees and their supervisors is used to evaluate and refine the training program.

Criteria 8.5:   Improvements and changes to initial and continuing training are systematically initiated, evaluated, tracked, and incorporated to track training deficiencies and performance problems.

E. DOE RCS, Article 613.7

Article 613.7 states:

Verification of the effectiveness of radiological control training should be accomplished by surveying a limited subset of former students in the workplace. This verification is in addition to performance evaluations routinely performed by training departments. This evaluation should include observation of practical applications and discussions of the course material and may include written examinations. The survey should be performed by radiological control managers and supervisors, quality assurance personnel, or senior instructors after the former student has had the opportunity to perform work for several months. The results should be documented.

F. Elements of Article 613.7

The following elements are stated:

1. The purpose of the evaluation is to verify the effectiveness of radiological control training.
2. The survey should be made on a subset of students several months after the training.
3. The survey may be conducted by training or nontraining personnel.
4. The survey should be conducted at the workplace.
5. The survey should be conducted in addition to any evaluations made as part of the training process.
6. The survey should consist of:
   - Observation of practical applications of the training;
   - Discussion of the course material with the trainee; and
   - An optional written examination, as appropriate, to measure retention.
7. The results should be documented.

G. Qualifications of Evaluators

Personnel who perform the evaluations should be technical experts on radiological control practices and should possess, or be trained to develop, interviewing skills and observational skills.

H. Correlation Between Evaluation and Training

The radiological control core training courses are nationally standardized. Any changes to the training materials, including the test banks, should be correlated by training oversight groups. How that correlation will be conducted is described in the program management guides for the courses.

Site specific radiological control training may be evaluated and revised by that site.

I. Training Requirements Based on Employee Duties

Table 3-1 of the RCS displays the types of workers and the recommended level of radiological training.

J. Stakeholder Consensus

Effective evaluation of training can only be conducted in a climate of consensus by all stakeholders. An essential element in the evaluation process is the development of consensus in advance of the evaluation. This involves agreement on the objectives of the evaluation, methods of evaluation to be used, and the required level of support that can be provided. Agreement should also be reached on whether the evaluation process will undergo the same approval cycle as that of other training materials.

Note that it may not be possible to obtain the same level of consensus in the development of a retention testing program, as the results of this program are used to provide remedial training for individuals exhibiting performance deficiencies. The retention testing program must be conducted in a manner that eliminates questions as to the fairness and unbiased manner in which the program is implemented.

K. A Checklist for Establishing and Implementing a Post-Training Evaluation Program

The following steps are essential in formalizing the post-training evaluation process and should be considered in developing site procedures:

1. Formalization via procedures of radiological control post-training evaluation;
2. Establishment of evaluation goals, objectives, and schedule, including building consensus among stakeholders;
3. Qualification of evaluators;
4. Preparation of evaluation materials;
5. Conduct of evaluations;
6. Reporting evaluation results; and
7. Program revision as applicable.

Note that this checklist is also applicable to a retention testing program.

II. PROGRAM ADMINISTRATION

A. Schedules For Conducting Post-Training Evaluation and Retention Testing

DOE suggests that, based on predicted proficiencies, post-training evaluation be scheduled 3 to 6 months following the training. Conducting the evaluation at least 3 months following the training would provide an opportunity for the trainee to have used the skills on the job. Site specific conditions may make it desirable to extend the period between training and evaluation, but data to support the extension decision should be collected to assure that the purposes of the evaluation are being met.

Note that this schedule is also applicable to a retention testing program.

B. Sample Sizes

The subset of former students to be sampled should be large enough to provide valid and reliable data for meeting the needs of the training and radiological control organizations. The number selected to be evaluated depends on the degree of precision and reliability desired.

Individuals to be evaluated should be selected using random number tables or some other randomizing technique unless the population size is so small that the randomizing effort will be of no value.

Table 1 is a matrix that describes a suggested level of sample size that can provide an appropriate level of comfort and can be used to establish the sample sizes to be used at each site. The percentages are based on the information provided in Dr. N.M. Dixon's *Evaluations: A Tool for HRD Quality.*"

Note that these sample size guidelines also apply to a retention testing program.

Table 1
Determining Sample Size for Post-Training Evaluations and Retention Testing

Percentage of trainees to be evaluated	1-40	41-100	101-160	161-250	251-380	381-600	601-900	901-1600	1601-3500	Over 3500
90-100%	X									
80-890%		X								
70-79%			X							
60-69%				X						
50-59%					X					
40-49%						X				
30-39%							X			
20-29%								X		
10-19%									X	
3-9%										X

C. Interpreting Results

Interpretation of results should be based on the original purpose(s) for conducting the evaluation. Interpretations can be centered on questions to be asked of the data. Table 2 shows samples of the type of questions that could be asked for each of the four purposes for evaluating training.

TABLE 2
Interpreting Evaluation Results

Purpose for Evaluation	Questions to Ask of Data
To measure the retention of skills and knowledge provided during training for extended periods following the training.	a. What is the average percentage of retention? b. What is the range of retention (highest and lowest)? c. Which objectives (knowledge/skill) were best retained? Which were least retained? d. How frequently were the least retained knowledge/skills used on the job? e. How many trainees fell below minimum passing requirements for the class? Why? f. What other variables, such as additional training, might have had an impact on retention?
To measure the degree to which training is used on the job.	a. How frequently is the knowledge/skill from training used on the job? b. Does the way in which a task is taught in training match exactly the way in which it is performed on the job? c. How is management/supervision reinforcing the knowledge/skills taught in the training at the worksite?
To provide feedback to improve the training.	a. Which knowledge/skill is not being used on the job? Why? b. If knowledge/skill is not retained, but is essential to job function, how can training make the learning of that skill more job like? c. What is the opinion of trainees regarding the benefits of the training after the extended time period? d. Were the training materials retained by the trainee after the class, and were they helpful as references back at the worksite? e. Have the trainees made any contact with instructors since the class for assistance? For what purpose? Was the contact helpful? f. What knowledge/skills need expanded or additional training?

TABLE 2 (continued)
Interpreting Evaluation Results

Purpose for Evaluation	Questions to Ask of Data
To measure the cost effectiveness of the training.	a. What is the actual cost of delivering this training? b. Do the data suggest that trainees were not positively affected by the training? How? c. Is the knowledge/skill provided by the training directly related to the work the trainee performs? d. What percent improvement in job performance resulted from completion of the training?
To incorporate corrective actions into individual development plans based on deficiencies observed during the retention testing process.	a. What percentage of other individuals performed satisfactorily in retention testing? b. How frequently were the unretained skills used on the job? c. How much remedial training has the individual already received? d. What changes have occurred that resulted in the individual completing original training, but failing retention testing? e. How critical to the individuals job function were the deficient items identified in retention training? f. What is the likelihood that enhanced training will result in improving the individuals performance to an acceptable level?

III. GUIDELINES FOR COURSE POST-TRAINING EVALUATION AND RETENTION TESTING

A. General Instructions

It may be beneficial and appropriate at some sites to combine in-field practical exams with training content discussions. Thus, the observer can pose the identified questions while observing actual work being performed.

1. **In-Field Observation:**

Five skill areas could be included in in-field observations: prejob preparations, knowledge level, radiological practices, emergency response practices, and exit practices. A checklist could be developed using a weighted point value system and identifying critical practices. The checklist could be modified to fit individual site requirements.

2. **Discussion Questions:**

Discussion with employees should determine whether the knowledge acquired in the training has been transferred to the job. The intent is not simply to measure retention of specific facts. The depth of the discussion would be directly correlated to the level of radiological hazard that may be encountered on the job.

3. **Written Exam:**

Written exams for evaluation of training effectiveness are optional.

These written exams may test retention of specific content from the courses. It may be desirable to use written tests that measure the ability to apply the knowledge from the training. In that instance, questions could be developed to measure student reaction to case studies. Such case study questions would allow each site to tailor the testing to its particular facilities, procedures, practices, and conditions.

B. GERT

1. **In-Field Observation:**

Some sites may desire to survey GERT trainees to determine their knowledge of hazardous areas to avoid. Awareness drills, such as placing mock radioactive material in an unauthorized location to assess responses are also effective.

2. **Discussion Questions:**

GERT trained employees access controlled areas. They should be aware of the hazards they may face in an emergency and how they should respond to those hazards. The following questions may be part of the discussion:

a. How many millirem of dose do you normally receive on your job in a year?
b. What is your annual dose limit; administrative dose guideline; when was the last time it was reported?
c. What types of radiation hazards exist at your facility?
d. How do you practice As Low As Reasonably Achievable (ALARA) in your work?
e. What are the sounds of the emergency alarms for your workplace?
f. How are employees at your work area warned of radiation hazards?
g. What obligations do you have to maintain exposure to radiation ALARA?

> h. What is dosimetry and what precautions should be taken when handling dosimeters?
>
> i. What radiological training are you required to take? How does your training relate to your job?

3. **Written Exam:**

   GERT trained employees are not required to pass a written examination.

C. RW I

1. **In-Field Observation:**

   Table 3 is a sample chart that illustrates the in-field activities and weighting system that could be used to observe RW I trainees. The numbers shown are based on conditions and priorities at a particular DOE site. Other sites may determine a different weighting system. Sites could choose to develop scenarios or drills in which to conduct in-field observations, or simply observe workers in their normal working environments.

TABLE 3
Sample RW I In-Field Observations Chart

ITEM EVALUATED	POINT VALUE	SCORE
Stated purpose of entry	2	
Stated radiation levels (w/units)	6	
Stated special instructions listed on radiological work permit (RWP)	6	
Selected dosimeters in accordance with RWP	4	
Dosimeters worn in accordance with procedures	4	
Recorded appropriate information on the RWP prior to entry	4	
Entered only areas designated on the RWP	3	
Followed special instructions (i.e., material to be taken into the radiological areas, etc.)	9	

Practiced ALARA (time, distance, shielding)	18	
Completed task as per RWP	9	
Stated appropriate actions to take when a radiation monitor alarmed	5	
Verified survey instrument in operation	5	
Surveyed for contamination properly (probe speed/distance, return probe to position)	12	
Resurveyed area when needed	4	
Stated proper actions to take if survey instrument should alarm	5	
Verified survey instrument in operation	4	
Significant mistake not identified by individual: Action involves violating instructions that lead to spread of contamination outside designated boundaries, or of unnecessary exposure to worker, jeopardizing personnel safety or creating a radiological hazard (eat, drink, chew, etc., in RCA). **AUTOMATIC FAILURE: DEDUCT 21 POINTS**		
COMMENTS:	100 Possible Score	___% Actual Score

2. **Discussion Questions:**

RW I personnel enter radiological buffer areas and radiation areas, but do not engage in activities requiring protective clothing. The following questions could be part of the discussion:

a. How many millirem of dose do you normally receive on your job in a year?
b. What is your annual dose limit; administrative dose guideline; when was the last time it was reported?
c. What types of radiation hazard exist at your facility?
d. What types of radiation are you exposed to in the course of your work? How do you protect yourself from these hazards?
e. How do you practice ALARA in your work?
f. What is the sound of continuous air monitor alarms for your workplace?
g. How are employees at your work area warned of radiation hazards?
h. What obligations do you have to maintain exposure to radiation ALARA?
i. What is dosimetry and what precautions should be taken when handling dosimeters?
j. What radiological training are you required to take? How does your training relate to your job?

3. **Written Exam:**

RW I training has recommended objectives for the core course plus any site specific objectives added for the site. The following approaches to retesting are being successfully applied throughout the DOE complex:

a. Conducting written retests twice each year on a sample of the trainees taught during the previous 6 months.
b. Retesting a sample of trainees 4 to 6 months following their training.
c. Retesting all objectives for a sample of trainees.
d. Retesting only those objectives that were found to be difficult for trainees to learn, remember, or apply in the previous 6 months.

Whichever pattern a site selects, the results should provide the data needed to meet the determined purposes of the evaluations.

D. RW II

1. **In-Field Observation:**

Table 4 shows a sample chart that illustrates the in-field activities and weighting system that could be used to observe RW II trainees. The numbers shown are based on conditions and priorities at a DOE site. Other sites may determine a different weighting system. Sites could choose to develop scenarios or drills in which to conduct in-field observations, or simply observe workers in their normal working environments.

TABLE 4
Sample RW II In-Field Observations Chart

ITEM EVALUATED	POINT VALUE	SCORE
Stated purpose of entry	3	
Stated radiation levels and contamination levels (with units)	5	
Selected protective clothing (PCs) and dosimeters in accordance with RWP	5	
Donned PCs properly	5	
Dosimeters worn in accordance with procedures	3	
Recorded appropriate information on the RWP prior to entry	5	
Entered only areas designated on the RWP	6	
Followed special instructions listed on the RWP	8	
Practiced ALARA (time, distance, shielding)	10	
Completed tasks as per RWP	6	
Removed PCs to minimize spread of contamination	10	
Placed items in proper receptacles upon doffing	5	
Verified survey instrument in operation	6	
Surveyed for contamination properly	10	
Stated appropriate actions for response to continuous air monitor alarm	8	
Recorded exposure on RWP upon exit	5	
Significant mistake not identified by individual: Action involving violating instructions that lead to spread of contamination outside designated		

boundaries, or of unnecessary exposure to worker, jeopardizing personnel safety or creating a radiological hazard (eat, drink, chew, etc., in RCA). **AUTOMATIC FAILURE: DEDUCT 21 POINTS**		
COMMENTS:	100 Possible Score	____% Actual Score

2.   **Discussion Questions:**

RW II personnel enter all radiological areas and engage in activities requiring protective clothing. The following questions could be part of the discussion:
   a.   How many millirem of dose do you normally receive on your job in a year?
   b.   What is your annual dose limit; administrative dose guideline; when was the last time it was reported?
   c.   What types of radiological hazards exist at your facility?
   d.   What types of radiation are you exposed to in the course of your work? How do you protect yourself from these hazards?
   e.   How do you practice ALARA in your work?
   f.   What is the sound of continuous air monitor alarms for your workplace?
   g.   How are employees at your work area warned of radiological hazards?
   h.   What obligations do you have to maintain exposure to radiation ALARA?
   i.   What is dosimetry? What precautions should be taken when handling dosimeters?
   j.   What practices do you take to assure you do not spread contamination while donning or doffing PCs?
   k.   What radiological training are you required to take? How does your training relate to your job?

3. **Written Exam:**

RW II training has recommended objectives for the core course plus any site specific objectives added for the site. Several approaches to retesting are being successfully applied throughout the DOE complex, as described for the RW I course.

Whichever pattern a site selects, the results should provide the data needed to meet the determined purposes of the evaluations.

E.   RCT Training

1. **In-Field Observation:**

RCT training consists of several phases. In Phase I, core lessons teach academic theory. Different sites have organized and emphasized the information in different ways to fit the needs and practices at the sites. In Phase II, practical skills are taught based on a site specific job assessment.

One difficulty in performing on-the-job observations is correlating the schedule of the observer with the schedule of the trainee. One approach to resolving this problem is to associate specific skills or tasks learned in the training with work evolutions that normally occur at the site.

Table 5 lists the tasks that will commonly appear in Phase II training in the left-hand column. The top row lists work evolutions where these tasks might be observed. A matrix could be prepared by marking an "X" in a box to show that a particular task can be observed in a particular evolution. The matrix could then be used to correlate with the procedures governing that evolution or task. An alternative is to prepare a checklist to use during the observation. Table 6 shows a sample of such a checklist.

TABLE 5
RCT Performance Tasks Cross-Referenced to Work Evolutions

WORK EVOLUTIONS PERFORMED IN THE FIELD

PERFORMANCE TASKS	Air Sampling	Contamination and Radiation Survey	Personnel and Material Release Survey	Use of Counter-Scaler Equipment	Personnel Decontamination	Equipment Decontamination	Access and Radioactive Source Control
AIR SAMPLING TASKS GROUP							
Draw and field count a grab sample							
Calculate the activity of a grab air sample							
Calculate a continuous air monitor (CAM) unit alarm setpoint							
Perform a background check of a CAM							
Perform CAM source/ efficiency check							
Conduct an air sample media exchange							
CONTAMINATION MONITORING TASKS GROUP							
Perform preoperational checks of contamination monitoring instrumentation							
Perform a removable contamination survey							
Perform a gross large area smear contamination survey							
Perform a direct contamination survey							
Document contamination survey results							
RADIATION MONITORING SKILLS GROUP							
Perform preoperational checks of radiation monitoring instrumentation							
Perform a general area dose rate survey							
Perform a contact dose rate survey							
Document radiation survey results							
COUNTER-SCALER EQUIPMENT TASKS GROUP							
Perform counter-scaler preoperational checks							
Field count a sample with the counter-scaler							
PROTECTIVE EQUIPMENT TASKS GROUP							
Don anticontamination clothing							
Remove							

anticontamination clothing						
HAZARDS POSTING TASKS GROUP						
Post an area to reflect hazards						
Repost an area						
Document posting changes/updates						
PERSONNEL DECONTAMINATION TASKS GROUP						
Perform skin/hair decontamination						
Perform personal effects decontamination						
Perform nasal smears						
RADIOACTIVE SOURCES TASKS GROUP						
Perform an inventory of radioactive sources						
Leak check radioactive sources						
Document radioactive source inventory/leak check						
DOCUMENTATION TASKS GROUP						
Complete field logbook entry						
Complete a request for procedure change						
Complete a Radiological Problem Report form						

TABLE 6
Sample RCT Field Observation Guide

RCT FIELD OBSERVATION GUIDE #123

EVOLUTION: Personnel Release Survey

Instructions to Field Observer

Brief the subject RCT prior to commencing the field observation to relieve concerns about being observed.

Participant must perform the task without help. A debriefing after the completion of the evolution may be appropriate to reinforce good habits and to correct weaknesses.

PERFORM PERSONNEL RELEASE SURVEYS
Perform a self survey or a survey of an individual for personnel release using portable contamination monitoring instrumentation.

Make comments in the section at the end of this document. Use the reference number associated with each of the skills listed below.	1 Inadequate	3 Adequate	5 Outstanding
1. Was the type or level of survey performed as called out by the Radiological Work Permit or other procedure?			
2. Was it verified by the RCT that daily preoperational checks on the instrument(s) had been completed?			
3. Was a preuse function check of the instrument performed?			
4. Did the RCT determine the background radiation level prior to commencing the personnel release survey?			
5. Did the RCT hold the instrument probe at the proper distance?			
6. Did the RCT scan for contamination at the proper speed?			
7. While surveying, did the RCT monitor for an audible increase in count rate above background?			
*** **IF Contamination was discovered** ***	-	-	-
8. Was Radiological Control supervision notified as required?			
9. Was a thorough whole-body survey of the individual performed?			
10. Was the event documented in accordance with prescribed procedures?			
11. If the individual was confirmed to be contaminated, were the recommended steps taken to preclude the spread of contamination and to proceed to a decontamination facility? Describe the actions taken in the comments section at the end of this document.			
NOTE: If personnel decontamination will be performed, see RCT Field Observation Guide #XYZ.			

COMMENTS (List by reference number)

2.   **Discussion Questions:**

RCTs support radiological work and engage in all activities in radiological areas. The following questions could be part of the discussion:

a. How many millirems of dose do you normally receive on your job in a year?
b. What is your annual dose limit? Administrative dose guideline; when was the last time it was reported?
c. What types of radiological hazards exist at your facility?
d. What types of radiation are you exposed to in the course of your work? How do you protect yourself from these hazards?
e. How do you practice ALARA in your work?
f. What is the sound of continuous air monitor alarms for your workplace?
g. How are employees at your work area warned of radiological hazards?
h. What are the biological symptoms you might display with increasing exposures to radiation?
i. What obligations do you have to maintain exposure to radiation ALARA?
j. What is dosimetry? What precautions should be taken when handling dosimeters?
k. What practices do you take to assure you do not spread contamination while donning or doffing PCs?
l. What radiological training are you required to take? How does your training relate to your job?

3.   **Written Exam:**

Each site should determine critical objectives to be retested for each lesson or class. Consideration should be given to the likelihood of a trainee having the opportunity to apply the skills from the training in an actual work environment. If the trainee is in training for an extended period of time, 2 to 4 months may pass without having had the opportunity to use the skills in actual work.

IV.   REFERENCES

The following materials provide a wide range of detailed data regarding principles and practices in evaluating training and will be useful for those desiring a more in-depth understanding of the evaluation process.

Dixon, Nancy M., "*Evaluations: A Tool for HRD Improvement*," University Associates, Inc. in Association with the American Society for Training and Development, San Diego, California, 1990.

"*Guidelines For Evaluation of Nuclear Facility Training Programs*," DOE-STD-1070-94 U.S. Department of Energy, Washington, D.C., Reaffirmed 1999.

Kirkpatrick, Donald L., "*Evaluating Training Programs*," American Society for Training and Development, Alexandria, Virginia, 1975.

Kirkpatrick, Donald L., "*More Evaluating Training Programs*," American Society for Training and Development, Alexandria, Virginia, 1987.

Newby, A.C., *"Evaluation Training Handbook*," Pfeiffer & Company, San Diego, California, 1992.

Phillips, Jack J., "*Handbook of Training Evaluation and Measurement Methods*," Gulf Publishing Company, Houston, Texas, 1983.

Robinson, Dana Gaines and James C., "*Training For Impact*," Jossey-Bass, Inc., San Francisco, California, 1989.

General Employee Radiological Training

Instructor's Guide

Coordinated and Conducted
for
Office of Environment, Safety & Health
U.S. Department of Energy

This page intentionally left blank.

Course Developers

Christine Liner	Savannah River Site
Al Reeder	Lockheed Martin Energy Systems
Carolyn Owen	Lawrence Livermore National Laboratory
Dean Atchinson	Brookhaven National Laboratory
Brent Pearson	Coleman Industries
Roland Jean	Sandia National Laboratory
Karin Jessen	Lockheed Martin Energy Systems

Course Reviewers

Technical Standards Managers	U.S. Department of Energy
Peter O'Connell	U.S. Department of Energy
William Ulicny	ATL International, Inc.

This page intentionally left blank.

Table of Contents

This page intentionally left blank

TERMINAL GOAL:

Upon completion of this training, the participant will be able to DISCUSS (1) the hazards associated with radiological areas and radioactive material, (2) his/her limitations as a trained general employee during access to or work in the controlled areas, and (3) his/her responsibilities for complying with radiological requirements, including his/her expected response to abnormal radiological events or emergencies.

ENABLING OBJECTIVES:

The participant will be able to:

EO1   IDENTIFY basic radiological fundamentals and radiation protection concepts.

EO2   IDENTIFY the relative risks of exposure to radiation and radioactive materials, including prenatal radiation exposure.

EO3   IDENTIFY physical design features, controls, limits, policies, procedures, alarms, and other measures implemented at the facility to control doses.

EO4   IDENTIFY individual rights and responsibilities as related to implementation of the radiation protection program (including the ALARA Program).

EO5   IDENTIFY actions implemented to control doses under emergency conditions.

EO6   IDENTIFY exposure reports or other exposure data which may be provided and how to request these reports.

Prerequisites:

None

General Employee Radiological Training   Instructor's Guide

I.   LESSON INTRODUCTION

A. Self Introduction
1.   Name
2.   Phone Number
3.   Background

B. Course Overview

General Employee Radiological Training (GERT) is provided to all site employees who receive occupational exposure during access to controlled areas at a DOE site or facility or who are permitted unescorted access to controlled areas. These individuals may routinely enter the controlled area and encounter radiological barriers, postings, radiation producing devices or radioactive materials. Employee responsibilities for observing and obeying radiological postings and procedures are emphasized throughout this training.

Additional training beyond GERT is required for the employees who are identified as radiological workers. Every employee, both radiological worker and non-radiological worker, must play an active part in maintaining exposures to radiation and radioactive materials within DOE limits and As Low As Is Reasonably Achievable (ALARA).

OPTIONAL:
Discuss and/or display various signs that the worker may be familiar with (e.g., road signs, restroom signs, no smoking signs, etc.) and site specific signs they may encounter on the job.

Discuss:
Relate the responsibilities associated with road signs to responsibilities with radiological postings.

General Employee Radiological Training　　　　　　　Instructor's Guide

GERT qualified individuals should be able to place the risks associated with working at a nuclear facility in perspective with other risks that we take in our everyday life.

List examples of other activities that have risks (e.g., smoking, driving a car, eating fatty foods, etc.) The risks from these activities will be discussed later.

C.　Introduce Objectives

　　1.　Terminal Goal
　　2.　Enabling Objectives

II.　LESSON

A.　Non-ionizing and Ionizing Radiation (EO1)

EO1 - IDENTIFY basic radiological fundamentals and radiation protection concepts.

Radiation is energy emitted through space and matter. This energy release is in the form of rays or particles and is emitted from unstable atoms or various radiation-producing devices, such as televisions and X-ray machines.

1.　Atoms

The elements that make up all matter are composed of atoms. Atoms have three basic particles; protons, neutrons and electrons.

a.　Stable atoms

Most atoms are stable and do not emit excess energy.

b.　Unstable atoms

Unstable atoms emit excess energy. This energy is called radiation.

2. Ionizing radiation

    Ionizing radiation has enough
    energy to remove electrons from
    electrically neutral atoms.

    - There are four basic types of
      ionizing radiation; alpha
      particles, beta particles,
      neutrons and gamma rays.

Note: X-rays are identical to gamma rays except for their place of origin. X-rays originate from a shell electron and gamma rays originate from the nucleus of an atom.

3. Non-ionizing radiation

    Non-ionizing radiation does not have
    enough energy to remove an
    electron from an atom.

    - Types of non-ionizing radiation
      include: Microwaves, radio
      waves, visible light, heat, and
      infrared radiation.

    Non-ionizing radiation is not
    addressed further in this training.

Insert facility-specific information if hazardous non-ionizing radiation sources are present.

OPTIONAL: Draw/show example of electromagnetic spectrum. Explain that these are all radiation, but have different energy levels. (Relate this concept by comparing microwaves/radio waves/visible light).

4. Radioactive Contamination

    Contamination is uncontained
    radioactive material in an unwanted
    location.

5. Comparison of radiation and
    radioactive contamination

    Exposure to radiation does <u>NOT</u>
    result in contamination of the worker.
    Only in the case of an individual
    coming in contact with radioactive
    contamination would there be a
    potential for the individual's skin or
    clothing to become contaminated.

Use example(s), such as a camp fire or powdered donuts, to depict the concept of radiation vs. contamination.

4

B. Sources of Radiation (EO1)

People have always been exposed to radiation. Radiation, simply defined, is energy emitted through space and matter. We are exposed to radiation from naturally-occurring sources in our environment, man-made sources, and even from materials inside our bodies.

- The average annual radiation dose to a member of the general population is about 360 millirem/year. This amount is a combination of both natural background and man-made sources of radiation.

1. Natural background sources of radiation

   Natural background radiation is by far the largest contributor (about 300 millirem/year) to radiation doses. The main sources of natural background radiation are listed below:

   a. Cosmic radiation - radiation from the sun and outer space, varies with altitude, (e.g., Denver would be higher than Miami).

   b. Radon - (the principal source of background radiation exposure.) A gas from naturally-occurring uranium in the soil.

   c. Terrestrial radiation from naturally- occurring radioactive material found in the earth's crust, such as uranium found in rocks and soil.

EO1 - IDENTIFY basic radiological fundamentals and radiation protection concepts.

OPTIONAL:
Explain that just as the inch is a basic unit to measure distance, the rem is the basic unit of measure used to equate the amount of potential biological damage done to our bodies by radiation. (1 rem = 1000 millirem)

    d. Materials present in <u>our bodies</u>. These come from naturally-occurring radioactive material present in our food, such as Potassium-40.

2. Man-made sources of radiation

    Man-made sources of radiation, where the radiation is either produced or enhanced by human activities, contribute to the remainder of the annual average radiation dose (approximately 60 millirem). Man-made sources include the following:

    a. Medical uses such as X rays and nuclear medicine tests or treatments

    b. Tobacco products

    c. Building materials

3. Comparison of annual radiation doses from selected sources

    Examples of the annual radiation dose (mrem) from selected sources of radiation exposure are as follows:

Note that these are average figures and can vary significantly depending on the individual's location and specific attributes associated with the exposure.

- Cigarette smoking (1 pack a day) 1300   1300

- Radon 200

- Medical exposures (average) 54   54

- Terrestrial radiation (rocks and soil) 28

- Cosmic radiation (sun and space) 28

- Round trip US by air 5

- Building materials 7

- World wide fallout <1

- Domestic water
  supply 5

- Natural gas range 0.2

- Smoke detectors 0.001

C.   Risks in Perspective (EO2)

Radiation comes from background and man-made sources. We receive approximately 360 millirem/year. This is separate from occupational exposure. In addition, radiation dose may also be received on the job. The potential risks from this exposure can be compared to other risks we accept everyday.

EO2 - IDENTIFY the relative risks of exposure to radiation and radioactive materials, including prenatal radiation exposure.

1. Occupational dose

   The risks associated with occupational doses are very small and considered acceptable when compared to that of other occupational health risks (i.e., being a coal miner or construction worker).

OPTIONAL:
Include the most recent average annual radiation dose for non-radiological workers and radiological workers at the site.

   a. Radiation dose limit (EO3)

      The DOE whole body radiation dose limit for general employees is 5000 millirem/year.

EO3 - IDENTIFY physical design features, controls, limits, policies, procedures, alarms, and other measures implemented at the facility to control doses.

b. Administrative Control Levels

Sites typically have administrative control levels below the DOE limit. (Insert facility-specific limits). Individuals who complete only this GERT training are not expected to receive more than 100 millirem/yr occupational dose.

c. Average annual radiation dose for various occupations

DOE radiological workers who received measurable radiological doses had an average dose of less than 75 millirem in 2001. This amount is compared to other occupations.

Occupation (millirem/year)
*   Airline flight crew member 400-600
*   Nuclear power plant worker 300
*   DOE/DOE contractors 75
*   Medical personnel 70

2. Potential health effects from exposure to radiation. (EO2)

Biological effects from exposure to radiation <u>may</u> occur in the exposed individual or in the future children of the exposed individual.

EO2 - IDENTIFY the relative risks of exposure to radiation and radioactive materials, including prenatal radiation exposure.

a.   Exposed individual

> There is scientific evidence for health effects (primarily cancer) from radiation doses well above the annual limit for occupational exposure (greater than 10,000 millirem). The risks associated with occupational doses are very small and considered acceptable when compared to other occupational risks.

> For very large doses received over a short period of time, prompt effects (i.e., effects that appear shortly after the exposure) may result. These doses are received typically under accident conditions such as the firefighters responding to the Chernobyl accident. These effects may include reddening of the skin, vomiting, hair loss, or even death.

       b.   Future children of the exposed individual

> Heritable effects (i.e., genetic changes to the parents sperm and/or eggs that results in an observed effect in their offspring) from ionizing radiation have been found in plants and animals, but have not been observed in human populations.

OPTIONAL: The current rate of cancer deaths in the US from all causes is ~20%. Many things can cause cancer, including high exposures to radiation. A 25,000 millirem dose would result in an increased risk of cancer from 20% (background rate) to 21%.

The risk of heritable effects from ionizing radiation is considered to be very small when compared to other naturally-occurring heritable effects and difficult to detect over the natural background rate of birth defects.

3. Prenatal effects (EO2)

EO2 - IDENTIFY the relative risks of exposure to radiation and radioactive materials, including prenatal radiation exposure.

A developing embryo/fetus is especially sensitive to ionizing radiation. Radiation is one of many agents that may cause harm to the embryo/fetus (i.e., chemicals, heat, etc.). Significant radiation doses (>10,000 millirem) to the embryo/fetus may increase the chances that the child will develop conditions such as a small head size, lower birth weight, and/or slower mental growth.

a. Possible effects

Radiation dose to the embryo/fetus may increase the chances that the child will develop conditions such as slower growth or mental development or childhood cancer. These effects can also be caused by many other hazards in our environment.

Optional: The natural rate of birth defects in the US is ~ 11%. A 25,000 millirem dose to the fetus/embryo may increase the chance of a birth defect from 11% to 11.1%.

DISCUSS declared pregnant worker.

b. DOE Limits (EO2)

The risk of these effects occurring is minimized by having special protective measures for the embryo/fetus of a declared pregnant women. The limit for the embryo/fetus is 500 millirem for the period from conception to birth.

1) A worker may voluntarily notify her employer, in writing, when she is pregnant.

2) It is the recommendation of DOE's Radiological Control Standard that the employer provide the option for a reassignment of work tasks to a declared pregnant worker, without loss of pay or promotional opportunity, such that further occupational radiation exposure is unlikely.

4. Comparison of risks of occupational radiation doses with other health risks (EO2)

The risk of working with or around sources of ionizing radiation can be compared to the risks we accept as part of everyday life.

These data address the expected effect on the average life span of a large population of individuals subjected to the risk factor/behavior in question.

EO2 - IDENTIFY the relative risks of exposure to radiation and radioactive materials, including prenatal radiation exposure.

Note: Explain that there are ongoing scientific discussions concerning the validity of extrapolating high dose data to these very low numbers. The real risk may actually be significantly lower.

a. Loss of life expectancy due to various causes (Expressed in days)

       <u>Health Risk and Estimated Days of Life Expectancy</u>

- Being unmarried male
  3500 days
- Smoking (1 pack/day)
  2250 days
- Being unmarried female
  1600 days
- Being a coal miner
  1100 days
- 15% overweight
  777 days
- Alcohol (US average)
  365 days
- Being a construction worker
  227 days
- Driving a motor vehicle
  205 days
- All industry
  60 days
- Radiation 100 mrem/yr
  (for 70 yr) 10 days
- Coffee (US Average)
  6 days

b. The following activities create a risk of 1 in a million chances of dying

- Smoking 1.4 cigarettes (lung cancer)
- Eating 40 tablespoons of peanut butter
- Eating 100 charcoal broiled steaks
- Spending 2 days in New York City (air pollution)

- Driving 40 miles in a car (accident)
- Flying 2500 miles in a jet (accident)
- Canoeing for 6 minutes
- Receiving 2.5 mrem of radiation (cancer) (based on extrapolation of the current DOE dose model)

5. Benefit versus risk (EO2)

    In summary, the estimated risk associated with occupational radiation dose, when compared to other occupational risks, is considered to be within the normal range of risk tolerance by national and international scientific groups who have studied these issues. Clearly though, the acceptance of risk is a personal matter that each individual must make for themselves and is best made with accurate information.

D. Radiological Controls (EO3)

Radiological controls are established to protect individuals from unplanned or uncontrolled exposure to radiation and from ingestion, inhalation, or absorption of radioactive material. These controls include, but are not limited to, a unique system of identifying radioactive materials using certain colors and/or symbols and radiological postings, implementation of controls to maintain radiation exposures As Low As Reasonably Achievable (ALARA), and training of workers on radiation safety and emergency response.

EO2 - IDENTIFY the relative risks of exposure to radiation and radioactive materials, including prenatal radiation exposure.

EO3 - IDENTIFY physical design features, controls, limits, policies, procedures, alarms, and other measures implemented at the facility to control doses.

1. Radiological identification system(s)

    Only especially trained/qualified
    workers are permitted to enter areas
    controlled for radiological purposes
    or handle radioactive material. All
    areas or material controlled for
    radiological purposes are identified
    by one or more of the following.

    a. Signs that have the standard
        radiation symbol colored
        magenta or black on a yellow
        background are used.

    b. Yellow and magenta rope, tape,
        chains or other barriers are used
        to designate the boundaries of
        posted areas.

    c. Tags and labels with a yellow
        background and either a
        magenta or black standard
        radiation symbol are used to
        identify radioactive material.
        "CAUTION-RADIOACTIVE
        MATERIAL"

    d. Yellow plastic wrapping, yellow
        plastic bags and labeled
        containers are used to package
        radioactive material.

    e. Designated areas are used to
        store radioactive material.

    f. Protective clothing used to
        prevent personnel contamination
        is yellow and/or distinctively
        marked.

    g. Potentially contaminated tools,
        and portable equipment used for
        radiological work are marked.

Show examples of radiological
signs, tags, clothing, etc

Show Symbol

Show Sign

Show Examples

NOTE: Show how anti-
contamination clothing is marked at
your facility.

14

2. Postings (EO3) Postings are used to alert personnel of a potential or known radiological condition and to aid them in controlling exposures and preventing the spread of contamination.	EO3 - IDENTIFY physical design features, controls, limits, policies, procedures, alarms, and other measures implemented at the facility to control doses.
a. Controlled Area Controlled areas are areas established around radiological areas to manage personnel access to the radiological areas and to provide warning of the existence of radiological hazards in the area. This training will permit you unescorted entry into the controlled area.	Show facility-specific sign for controlled area
b. Radioactive Material Area This is an area within a controlled area where radioactive material in excess of specified quantities is located. This training alone typically will not permit you unescorted access to these areas.	Show sign for radioactive material area. Discuss facility-specific access requirements.
c. Radiological Areas There are radiological areas established within the controlled area.	Show signs for areas.

"Radiation Area, High Radiation Area, and Very High Radiation Area," identify areas where the hazard is exposure to ionizing radiation and the different areas designate increasing levels of hazard (increasing levels of dose rates).

Discuss facility-specific access requirements.

"Contamination Area" and "High Contamination Area" identify areas where the hazard is from accessible loose radioactive contamination. Protective clothing is used to prevent contamination of personnel.

"Airborne Radioactivity Area" indicates the potential for radioactive contamination in the air. Protective clothing and respiratory protection may be used to protect personnel from inhaling the contamination or getting contamination on their skin."

This training typically will **NOT** permit you to enter these areas. Personnel trained at the GERT level are typically not permitted to enter these areas unless escorted and/or trained.

DISCUSS other facility-specific areas, such as soil contamination area.

d. Radiological Buffer Area

A radiological buffer area may be established within the controlled area to provide a secondary boundary for minimizing exposures to radiation or contamination.

(These are not required by 10 CFR 835). Show facility-specific sign for radiological buffer area.

This training typically does NOT qualify you to enter the radiological buffer area unless you are continuously escorted. (Insert facility-specific requirements.)

16

E. ALARA Program (EO4)

1. ALARA Concept

The DOE and this Site are firmly committed to having a Radiological Control Program of the highest quality. Therefore, maintaining occupational dose from radiation and radioactive materials As Low As Is Reasonably Achievable (ALARA) is an integral part of all site activities. The purpose of the ALARA program is to control radiation doses in consideration of the overall benefit of the activity causing the dose.

There are a few basic practices used to maintain exposure to radiation ALARA.

a. Time-Reduce the amount of time spent near a source of radiation.

b. Distance-Stay as far away from the source as possible.

c. Shielding-Shielding is placed between workers and the source.

d. Radioactive contamination is controlled using engineered ventilation, containments, decontamination, and lastly, PPE to minimize the potential for inhalation, ingestion, or absorption of radioactive material.

EO4 - IDENTIFY individual rights and responsibilities as related to implementation of the radiation protection program (including the ALARA Program.)

OPTIONAL:
Discuss the radiological control philosophy that there be no personnel dose without commensurate benefit.

OPTIONAL:
Discuss some facility-specific examples of each of these exposure control techniques.

F.   Emergency Procedures (EO5)

In the unlikely event that a radiological incident occurs, it is important for each employee to know the emergency procedures.

EO5 - IDENTIFY actions implemented to control doses under emergency conditions.

1.   Abnormal Conditions

If you discover radioactive material that is not where it belongs, (e.g., discarded in a clean trash receptacle, outside of radiological areas, or loose outside or in a building corridor), you should take the following actions:

Review examples of properly located and posted radioactive material.

a. Do not touch or handle the material.

b. Warn other personnel not to approach the area.

c. Guard the area, moving a safe distance, (see following ALARA Section) and have someone immediately notify Radiological Control personnel.

d. Await Radiological Control personnel.

These actions are taken to minimize exposure to radiation and potential contamination of yourself and others.

2.   Facility Alarms

(Insert facility specific information)

3.   Facility Evacuation Procedures

(Insert facility specific information)

G.   Employee Responsibilities (EO4)

All employees have an impact on maintaining exposures to radiation and radioactive material ALARA. Work planning is a key component of the ALARA program to ensure each of the controls listed below is applied as appropriate to the work being performed. Some of the employee responsibilities are listed.

EO4 - IDENTIFY individual rights and responsibilities as related to implementation of the radiation protection program (including the ALARA Program).

1.   Obey all signs/postings.

2.   Comply with all radiological and safety rules.

3.   Do not enter any radiological area unless escorted. If visiting a radiological area with an escort:

a. obey the instructions of your escort.

b. obtain and properly wear dosimeters as instructed by procedure, Radiological Control personnel, or your escort.

c. utilize ALARA techniques to control your exposure.

4.   Be alert for and report unusual radiological situations.

Unusual situations may include finding radioactive material outside a designated area or finding a compromised radiological barrier.

5. Know where and/or how to contact Radiological Control personnel in your work area.

6. Comply with emergency procedures for your work area.

7. Keep exposures to radiation and radioactive materials ALARA and know the Administrative Control Levels and Dose Limits.

8. Know your cumulative and annual dose.

H. Monitoring (Dosimetry)

Since radiation cannot be detected with the human senses, special detection devices must be used. Workers should become familiar with the equipment and devices used to measure and detect radiation and radioactive material, as applicable to their job functions. Monitoring is only required if you are likely to receive a dose in excess of 100 millirem in a year. Therefore, it is possible based on your job function and location that you will not be provided a dosimeter.

(Insert facility-specific information)

Some workers are monitored for intakes of radioactive material (e.g., inhaling or ingesting radioactive material). This is typically done by either using an apparatus (e.g., whole body counter) to detect the material or by analyzing a sample the individual provides (e.g., urinalysis).

Discuss/show dosimeters used at facility. Discuss any facility specific monitoring used for GERT trained employees.

I. Exposure Reports (EO6)

Although DOE and DOE contractor employees who are only trained at the GERT level are not expected to receive occupational dose above the monitoring threshold, they may be monitored for exposure in any case. This could occur during escorted entries into radiologically controlled areas or in other circumstances. Individuals who are monitored for exposure at DOE facilities have the right to request reports of that exposure as follows:

- Upon the request from an individual terminating employment, records of radiation exposure dose shall be provided by the DOE facility within 90 days. If requested, a written estimate of radiation exposure received by the terminating employee shall be provided at the time of termination.

- Each individual who is required to be monitored for radiation exposure at a DOE facility shall receive a report of that exposure on an annual basis.

Note: As previously discussed, individuals may be monitored with a dosimeter even though they are not required to be monitored. In this case an annual report is not required to be sent.

EO6 - IDENTIFY exposure reports or other exposure data that may be provided and how to request these reports.

- Detailed information concerning any individual's exposure shall be made available to the individual upon request of that individual.

- When a DOE contractor is required to report to the Department, pursuant to Departmental requirements for occurrence reporting and processing, any exposure of an individual to radiation and/or radioactive material, or planned special exposure, the contractor shall also provide that individual with a report on his/her exposure data included therein. Such a report shall be transmitted at a time not later than the transmittal to the Department.

III.   SUMMARY

It is important to understand what radiation and radioactive materials are and to recognize the postings associated with radiological work. All employees are responsible to comply with the safety rules and to access only areas they are authorized to enter. Through an enhanced awareness of this topic, each employee may contribute to safe practices in the workplace.

References:

1. DOE Radiological Control Standard [DOE-STD 1098-99]
2. "Guide to Good Practice in Radiation Protection Training," ORAU 88/H-99
3. US NRC Regulatory Guide 8.13, "Instruction Concerning Prenatal Radiation Exposure" December 1997
4. US NRC Regulatory Guide 8.29, "Instruction Concerning Risks from Occupational Radiation Exposure," July 1981
5. DOE Occupational Radiation Exposure 2001 Report, DOE/EH-0660
6. DOE 10 CFR 835, "Occupational Radiation Protection."

This page intentionally left blank.

General Employee Radiological Training

Student's Guide

**Coordinated and Conducted
for
Office of Environment, Safety & Health
U.S. Department of Energy**

This page intentionally left blank.

Course Developers

Christine Liner	Savannah River Site
Al Reeder	Lockheed Martin Energy Systems
Carolyn Owen	Lawrence Livermore National Laboratory
Dean Atchinson	Brookhaven National Laboratory
Brent Pearson	Coleman Industries
Roland Jean	Sandia National Laboratory
Karin Jessen	Lockheed Martin Energy Systems

Course Reviewers

Technical Standards Managers	U.S. Department of Energy
Peter O'Connell	U.S. Department of Energy
William Ulicny	ATL International, Inc

This page intentionally left blank.

Table of Contents

This page intentionally left blank.

TERMINAL GOAL:

Upon completion of this training, the participant will be able to DISCUSS (1) the hazards associated with radiological areas and radioactive material, (2) his/her limitations as a trained general employee during access to or work in the controlled areas, and (3) his/her responsibilities for complying with radiological requirements, including his/her expected response to abnormal radiological events or emergencies.

ENABLING OBJECTIVES:

The participant will be able to:

EO1 IDENTIFY basic radiological fundamentals and radiation protection concepts.

EO2 IDENTIFY the relative risks of exposure to radiation and radioactive materials, including prenatal radiation exposure.

EO3 IDENTIFY physical design features, controls, limits, policies, procedures, alarms, and other measures implemented at the facility to control doses.

EO4 IDENTIFY individual rights and responsibilities as related to implementation of the radiation protection program (including the ALARA Program).

EO5 IDENTIFY actions implemented to control doses under emergency conditions.

EO6 IDENTIFY exposure reports or other exposure data which may be provided and how to request these reports.

Prerequisites:

None

I. LESSON INTRODUCTION

A. Self Introduction

1. Name

2. Phone Number

3. Background

B. Course Overview

General Employee Radiological Training (GERT) is provided to all site employees who receive occupational exposure during access to controlled areas at a DOE site or facility or who are permitted unescorted access to controlled areas. These individuals may routinely enter the controlled area and encounter radiological barriers, postings, radiation producing devices or radioactive materials. Employee responsibilities for observing and obeying radiological postings and procedures are emphasized throughout this training.

- Additional training beyond GERT is required for the employees who are identified as radiological workers. Every employee, both radiological worker and non-radiological worker, must play an active part in maintaining exposures to radiation and radioactive materials within DOE limits and As Low As Is Reasonably Achievable (ALARA).

- GERT qualified individuals should be able to place the risks associated with working at a nuclear facility in perspective with other risks that we take in our everyday life.

C.   **Introduce Objectives**

    1. Terminal Goal

    2. Enabling Objectives

II.   **LESSON**

A. **Non-ionizing and Ionizing Radiation (EO1)**

    Radiation is energy emitted through space and matter. This energy release is in the form of rays or particles and is emitted from unstable atoms or various radiation-producing devices, such as televisions and X-ray machines.

    1. Atoms

        The elements that make up all matter are composed of atoms. Atoms have three basic particles: protons, neutrons and electrons.

        a. Stable atoms

            Most atoms are stable and do not emit excess energy

        b. Unstable atoms

            Unstable atoms emit excess energy. This energy is called radiation.

    2. Ionizing radiation

        Ionizing radiation has enough energy to remove electrons from electrically neutral atoms.

- There are four basic types of ionizing radiation; alpha particles, beta particles, neutrons and gamma rays.

3. Non-ionizing radiation

   Non-ionizing radiation does not have enough energy to remove an electron from an atom.

   - Types of non-ionizing radiation include: Microwaves, radio waves, visible light, heat, and infrared radiation.

   Non-ionizing radiation is not addressed further in this training.

4. Radioactive Contamination

   Contamination is uncontained radioactive material in an unwanted location.

5. Comparison of radiation and radioactive contamination

   Exposure to radiation does <u>NOT</u> result in contamination of the worker. Only in the case of an individual coming in contact with radioactive contamination would there be a potential for the individual's skin or clothing to become contaminated.

B. Sources of Radiation (EO1)

People have always been exposed to radiation. Radiation, simply defined, is energy emitted through space and matter. We are exposed to radiation from naturally-occurring sources in our environment, man-made sources, and even from materials inside our bodies.

- The average annual radiation dose to a member of the general population is about 360 millirem/year. This amount is a combination of both natural background and man-made sources of radiation.

1. Natural background sources of radiation

Natural background radiation is by far the largest contributor (about 300 millirem/year) to radiation doses. The main sources of natural background radiation are listed below:

a. Cosmic radiation - radiation from the sun and outer space, varies with altitude, (e.g., Denver would be higher than Miami).

b. Radon - (the principal source of background radiation exposure.) A gas from naturally-occurring uranium in the soil.

c. Terrestrial radiation from naturally-occurring radioactive material found in the earth's crust, such as uranium found in rocks and soil.

d. Materials present in our bodies. These come from naturally-occurring radioactive material present in our food, such as Potassium-40.

2. Man-made sources of radiation

Man-made sources of radiation, where the radiation is either produced or enhanced by human activities, contribute to the remainder of the annual average radiation dose (approximately 60 millirem). Man-made sources include the following:

a. Medical uses such as X-rays and nuclear medicine tests or treatments

b. Tobacco products

c. Building materials

3. Comparison of annual radiation doses from selected sources

Examples of the annual radiation dose from selected sources of radiation exposure are as follows:

- Cigarette smoking   1300
  (1 pack a day)

- Radon   200

- Medical exposures   54
  (average)

- Terrestrial radiation (rocks and soil)   28

- Cosmic radiation (sun and space)   28

- Round trip US by air   5

- Building materials   7

- World wide fallout   <1

- Domestic water supply   5

- Natural gas range   0.2

- Smoke detectors   0.001

C. Risks in Perspective (EO2)

Radiation comes from background and man-made sources. We receive approximately 360 millirem/year. This is separate from occupational exposure. In addition, radiation dose may also be received on the job. The potential risks from this exposure can be compared to other risks we accept everyday.

1. Occupational dose

   The risks associated with occupational doses are very small and considered acceptable when compared to that of other occupational health risks (i.e., being a coal miner or construction worker).

   a. Radiation dose limit (EO3)

      The DOE whole body radiation dose limit for general employees is 5000 millirem/year.

   b.   Administrative Control Levels

      Sites typically have administrative control levels below the DOE limit. (Insert facility-specific limits). Individuals who complete only this GERT training are not expected to receive more than 100 millirem/yr occupational dose.

   c. Average annual radiation dose for various occupations

DOE radiological workers who received measurable radiological doses had an average dose of less than 75 millirem in 2001. This amount is compared to other occupations.

Occupation	millirem/year
• Airline flight crew member	400-600
• Nuclear power plant worker	300
• DOE/DOE contractors	75
• Medical personnel	70

2. Potential health effects from exposure to radiation. (EO2)

Biological effects from exposure to radiation <u>may</u> occur in the exposed individual or in the future children of the exposed individual.

a. Exposed individual

There is scientific evidence for health effects (primarily cancer) from radiation doses well above the annual limit for occupational exposure (greater than 10,000 millirem). The risks associated with occupational doses are very small and considered acceptable when compared to other occupational risks.

For very large doses received over a short period of time, prompt effects (i.e., effects that appear shortly after the exposure) may result. These doses are received typically under accident conditions such as the firefighters responding to the Chernobyl accident. These effects may include reddening of the skin, vomiting, hair loss, or even death.

b. Future children of the exposed individual

Heritable effects (i.e., genetic changes to the parents sperm and/or eggs that results in an observed effect in their offspring) from ionizing radiation have been found in plants and animals, but have not been observed in human populations. The risk of heritable effects from ionizing radiation is considered to be very small when compared to other naturally-occurring heritable effects and difficult to detect over the natural background rate of birth defects.

3. Prenatal effects (EO2)

A developing embryo/fetus is especially sensitive to ionizing radiation. Radiation is one of many agents that may cause harm to the embryo/fetus (i.e., chemicals, heat, etc.). Significant radiation doses (>10,000 millirem) to the embryo/fetus may increase the chances that the child will develop conditions such as a small head size, lower birth weight, and/or slower mental growth.

a. Possible effects

Radiation dose to the embryo/fetus may increase the chances that the child will develop conditions such as slower growth or mental development or childhood cancer. These effects can also be caused by many other hazards in our environment.

b. DOE Limits (EO2)

The risk of these effects occurring is minimized by having special protective measures for the embryo/fetus of a declared pregnant women. The limit for the embryo/fetus is 500 millirem for the period from conception to birth.

1) A worker may voluntarily notify her employer, in writing, when she is pregnant.

2) It is the recommendation of DOE's Radiological Control Standard that the employer provide the option for a reassignment of work tasks to a declared pregnant worker, without loss of pay or promotional opportunity, such that further occupational radiation exposure is unlikely.

4. Comparison of risks of occupational radiation doses with other health risks (EO2)

> The risk of working with or around sources of ionizing radiation can be compared to the risks we accept as part of everyday life.

> These data address the expected effect on the average life span of a large population of individuals subjected to the risk factor/behavior in question.

a. Loss of life expectancy due to various causes (Expressed in days)

Health Risk	Estimated Days of Life Expectancy Lost, Average
Being unmarried male	3500
Smoking (1 pack/day)	2250
Being unmarried female	1600
Being a coal miner	1100
15% overweight	777
Alcohol (US average)	365
Being a construction worker	227
Driving a motor vehicle	205
All industry	60
Radiation 100 mrem/yr (70 yr)	10
Coffee (US Average)	6

13

b. The following activities create a risk of 1 in a million chances of dying

- Smoking 1.4 cigarettes (lung cancer)

- Eating 40 tablespoons of peanut butter

- Eating 100 charcoal broiled steaks

- Spending 2 days in New York City (air pollution)

- Driving 40 miles in a car (accident)

- Flying 2500 miles in a jet (accident)

- Canoeing for 6 minutes

- Receiving 2.5 mrem of radiation (cancer) (based on extrapolation of the current DOE dose model)

5. Benefit versus risk (EO2)

In summary, the estimated risk associated with occupational radiation dose, when compared to other occupational risks, is considered to be within the normal range of risk tolerance by national and international scientific groups who have studied these issues. Clearly though, the acceptance of risk is a personal matter that each individual must make for themselves and is best made with accurate information.

D. Radiological Controls (EO3)

Radiological controls are established to protect individuals from unplanned or uncontrolled exposure to radiation and from ingestion, inhalation, or absorption of radioactive material. These controls include, but are not limited to, a unique system of identifying radioactive materials using certain colors and/or symbols and radiological postings, implementation of controls to maintain radiation exposures As Low As Is Reasonably Achievable (ALARA), and training of workers on radiation safety and emergency response.

1. Radiological identification system(s)

    Only specially trained/qualified workers are permitted to enter areas controlled for radiological purposes or handle radioactive material. All areas or material controlled for radiological purposes are identified by one or more of the following.

    a. Signs that have the standard radiation symbol colored magenta or black on a yellow background are used.

    b. Yellow and magenta rope, tape, chains or other barriers are used to designate the boundaries of posted areas.

    c. Tags and labels with a yellow background and either a magenta or black standard radiation symbol are used to identify radioactive material.

    "CAUTION-RADIOACTIVE MATERIAL"

    d. Yellow plastic wrapping, yellow plastic bags and labeled containers are used to package radioactive material.

    e. Designated areas are used to store radioactive material.

    f. Protective clothing used to prevent personnel contamination is yellow and/or distinctively marked.

15

g. Potentially contaminated tools, and portable equipment used for radiological work are marked.

2. Postings (EO3)

Postings are used to alert personnel of a potential or known radiological condition and to aid them in controlling exposures and preventing the spread of contamination.

a. Controlled Area

1) Controlled areas are areas established around radiological areas to manage personnel access to the radiological areas and to provide warning of the existence of radiological hazards in the area.

2) This training will permit you unescorted entry into the controlled area.

b. Radioactive Material Area

1) This is an area within a controlled area where radioactive material in excess of specified quantities is located.

2) This training alone typically will not permit you unescorted access to these areas.

c. Radiological Areas

1) There are radiological areas established within the controlled area.

"Radiation Area, High Radiation Area, and Very High Radiation Area," identify areas where the hazard is exposure to ionizing radiation and the different areas designate increasing levels of hazard (increasing levels of dose rates).

"Contamination Area" and "High Contamination Area" identify areas where the hazard is from accessible loose radioactive contamination. Protective clothing is used to prevent contamination of personnel.

"Airborne Radioactivity Area" indicates the potential for radioactive contamination in the air. Protective clothing and respiratory protection may be used to protect personnel from inhaling the contamination or getting contamination on their skin."

2) This training typically will <u>NOT</u> permit you to enter these areas. Personnel trained at the GERT level are typically not permitted to enter these areas unless escorted and/or trained.

d. Radiological Buffer Area

1) A radiological buffer area may be established within the controlled area to provide a secondary boundary for minimizing exposures to radiation or contamination.

2) This training typically does NOT qualify you to enter the radiological buffer area unless you are continuously escorted. (Insert facility-specific requirements.)

E. ALARA Program (EO4)

1. ALARA Concept

The DOE and this Site are firmly committed to having a Radiological Control Program of the highest quality. Therefore, maintaining occupational dose from radiation and radioactive materials As Low As Is Reasonably Achievable (ALARA) is an integral part of all site activities. The purpose of the ALARA program is to control radiation doses in consideration of the overall benefit of the activity causing the dose.

There are a few basic practices used to maintain exposure to radiation ALARA.

a. Time-Reduce the amount of time spent near a source of radiation.

b. Distance-Stay as far away from the source as possible.

c. Shielding-Shielding is placed between workers and the source.

d. Radioactive contamination is controlled using engineered ventilation, containments, decontamination, and lastly, PPE to minimize the potential for inhalation, ingestion, or absorption of radioactive material.

F. Emergency Procedures (EO5)

In the unlikely event that a radiological incident occurs, it is important for each employee to know the emergency procedures.

1.   Abnormal Conditions

If you discover radioactive material that is not where it belongs, (e.g., discarded in a clean trash receptacle, outside of radiological areas, or loose outside or in a building corridor), you should take the following actions:

1) Do not touch or handle the material.

2) Warn other personnel not to approach the area.

3) Guard the area, moving a safe distance, (see following ALARA Section) and have someone immediately notify Radiological Control personnel.

4) Await Radiological Control personnel.

These actions are taken to minimize exposure to radiation and potential contamination of yourself and others.

2.   Facility Alarms

(Insert facility specific information)

19

3.   Facility Evacuation Procedures

(Insert facility specific information)

G. Employee Responsibilities (EO4)

All employees have an impact on maintaining exposures to radiation and radioactive material ALARA. Work planning is a key component of the ALARA program to ensure each of the controls listed below is applied as appropriate to the work being performed. Some of the employee responsibilities are listed.

1.   Obey all signs/postings.

2.   Comply with all radiological and safety rules.

3.   Do not enter any radiological area unless escorted. If visiting a radiological area with an escort:

   a.   obey the instructions of your escort.

   b.   obtain and properly wear dosimeters as instructed by procedure, Radiological Control personnel, or your escort.

   c.   utilize ALARA techniques to control your exposure.

4. Be alert for and report unusual radiological situations.

    Unusual situations may include finding radioactive material outside a designated area or finding a compromised radiological barrier.

5. Know where and/or how to contact Radiological Control personnel in your work area.

6. Comply with emergency procedures for your work area.

7. Keep exposures to radiation and radioactive materials ALARA and know the Administrative Control Levels and Dose Limits.

8. Know your cumulative and annual dose.

H. Monitoring (Dosimetry)

Since radiation <u>cannot</u> be detected with the human senses, special detection devices must be used. Workers should become familiar with the equipment and devices used to measure and detect radiation and radioactive material, as applicable to their job functions. Monitoring is only required if you are likely to receive a dose in excess of 100 millirem in a year. Therefore, it is possible based on your job function and location that you will not be provided a dosimeter.

(Insert facility-specific information)

Some workers are monitored for intakes of radioactive material (e.g., inhaling or ingesting radioactive material). This is typically done by either using an apparatus (e.g., whole body counter) to detect the material or by analyzing a sample the individual provides (e.g., urinalysis).

I. Exposure Reports (EO6)

Although DOE and DOE contractor employees who are only trained at the GERT level are not expected to receive occupational dose above the monitoring threshold, they may be monitored for exposure in any case. This could occur during escorted entries into radiologically controlled areas or in other circumstances. Individuals who are monitored for exposure at DOE facilities have the right to request reports of that exposure as follows:

•   Upon the request from an individual terminating employment, records of radiation exposure dose shall be provided by the DOE facility within 90 days. If requested, a written estimate of radiation exposure received by the terminating employee shall be provided at the time of termination.

•   Each individual who is required to be monitored for radiation exposure at a DOE facility shall receive a report of that exposure on an annual basis.

Note: As previously discussed, individuals may be monitored with a dosimeter even though they are not required to be monitored. In this case an annual report is not required to be sent.

• Detailed information concerning any individual's exposure shall be made available to the individual upon request of that individual.

• When a DOE contractor is required to report to the Department, pursuant to Departmental requirements for occurrence reporting and processing, any exposure of an individual to radiation and/or radioactive material, or planned special exposure, the contractor shall also provide that individual with a report on his/her exposure data included therein. Such a report shall be transmitted at a time not later than the transmittal to the Department.

III. SUMMARY

It is important to understand what radiation and radioactive materials are and to recognize the postings associated with radiological work. All employees are responsible to comply with the safety rules and to access only areas they are authorized to enter. Through an enhanced awareness of this topic, each employee may contribute to safe practices in the workplace.

References :

1. DOE Radiological Control Standard [DOE-STD 1098-99]
2. "Guide to Good Practice in Radiation Protection Training," ORAU 88/H-99
3. US NRC Regulatory Guide 8.13, "Instruction Concerning Prenatal Radiation Exposure" December 1997
4. US NRC Regulatory Guide 8.29, "Instruction Concerning Risks from Occupational Radiation Exposure," July 1981
5. DOE Occupational Radiation Exposure 2001 Report, DOE/EH-0660
6. DOE 10 CFR 835, "Occupational Radiation Protection."

CONCLUDING MATERIAL

Review Activities:

<u>DOE</u>	<u>Ops Offices</u>	<u>Field Offices</u>
DP	AL	RFSO
EH	CH	OH
EM	ID	GFO
ER	NV	
FM	OR	
LM	RL	
NE	SR	
NS		
PR		
SA		

Preparing Activity:

DOE EH-52: Peter O'Connell

Project Number:

TRNG-0001

<u>Area Offices</u>	<u>National Laboratories</u>
Amarillo	BNL
Ashtabula	LANL
Carlsbad	LLNL
Columbus	PNNL
Fernald	Sandia
Kansas City	FNL
Kirtland	
Los Alamos	
Miamisburg	
Pinellas	
West Valley